LUTON LIBRARIES

LUTON
BOROUGH COUNCIL

Published by
Amberwood Publishing Ltd
Park Corner, Park Horsley, East Horsley, Surrey KT24 5RZ
Tel: 01483 570821

PLANTLIFE

The Natural History Museum, Cromwell Road, London SW7 5BD

Registered Charity No. 328576

Amberwood Publishing supports the Plantlife Charity,
Britain's only charity exclusively dedicated to saving wild plants.

ISBN 1-899308-12-1

Typeset and designed by
Word Perfect, Christchurch, Dorset.

Cover design by Howland Northover

Printed in Great Britain

CONTENTS

About the Author

Ann Percival is a State Registered Nurse, Qualified Aromatherapist and Bach Flower Remedy Counsellor.

She started her nursing training at Paddington General (now St Mary's Hospital) and took up her first staff nurse post at Queen Mary's University Hospital, Roehampton on a male surgical ward, later transferring to the Psychiatric Day Hospital. Following the birth of her daughter Francesca she moved with her family to Gloucestershire.

Whilst studying aromatherapy she worked part time as a staff nurse on the Cardiology ward of her local NHS hospital, and was to later move to the Oncology Unit.

She has a successful private practise at Natural Therapeutics in Cheltenham, a specialist health care shop and clinic run by her husband. Additionally she is the in-house aromatherapist for a fund holding General Practice.

Ann has a keen interest in teaching. In addition to running her own classes, her experience includes teaching for her local adult education authority. She currently holds introductory courses on Aromatherapy and Massage.

Acknowledgements

Special thanks to Christabel Burniston for her warm encouragement, proofing the manuscript and writing the introduction.

This book is dedicated to my daughter Francesca

Note to Reader

Whilst the author has made every effort to ensure that the contents of this book are accurate in every particular, it is not intended to be regarded as a substitute for professional medical advice under treatment. The reader is urged to give careful consideration to any difficulties which he or she is experiencing with their own health and to consult their General Practitioner if uncertain as to its cause or nature. Neither the author nor the publisher can accept any legal responsibility for any health problem which results from use of the self-help methods described.

Introduction

Through her skills and sensibility, Ann Percival invites you to develop a friendship with Aromatherapy and the essential oils.

I have the pleasure of being her client, albeit irregularly. My profession involves time and travel away from home, but on those precious visits to Ann, I cast away work and worries, and relax into her hands. When I leave her clinic the whole world looks lighter, brighter and calmer.

But, if your visits to a professional practitioner have to be limited (time and money too often being the limiting factors) you can profit from Ann's generous advice and build up a personal collection of your own essential oils to use in the privacy of your home.

Like all sensible women you will, of course, have regular checks with your doctor and consult him, or her, if any doubt exists in your mind about any unusual symptom. In addition you will, I hope, visit a reputable and empathetic aromatherapist as often as you can afford the time and money.

Rest assured that any supportive help you give yourself through your own cosseting can only do good. Aromatherapy complements other treatments as the whole science (and it is a science) is based on healing and reinforcing the immune system.

May I conclude with a personal note? I have a highly complex professional life which includes problem-solving, consultations, travel, and speaking engagements. As with other women it is essential to feel relaxed and to look and sound enjoyably responsive.

It is no secret (for my birth date appears in the opening sentence of my recently published autobiography of childhood) that I am 86 and with a great deal of work ahead. Ann and aromatherapy will help to keep me 'on the road'.

Here's to your enjoyment of, and success with, Ann's splendid guide through which you can choose and use the essential and potent oils that are right for YOU.

Christabel Burniston MBE (Spring 1996)

1 | Essential oils: a precious possession

Essential oils are the potent and highly concentrated oils which are used in Aromatherapy. They are extracted or distilled from numerous plants, shrubs and trees and are found in special cells in the leaves, flowers, fruit, stems, barks, seeds, berries and rinds.

They are highly aromatic, volatile and non greasy. Essential oils dissolve in fatty oils such as grapeseed oil, sweet almond oil, avocado oil and many other plant oils. Essential oils are also soluble in alcohol. They do not dissolve in water. They are suspended in water and can be vaporised or used in water sprays, washes and compresses.

Essences are produced by special secretory cells in plants. They do not become an essential oil until after distillation. The amount of essence in a plant can vary, this is dependent upon factors such as soil conditions, weather and harvesting.

Each plant will contain hundreds of natural chemical constituents. It is the unique combination of constituents which gives an oil its individual perfume and therapeutic properties. The combination of chemicals acts in a synergistic way and aromatherapists are trained to blend essential oils for each individual whom they treat.

The extraction of oils

Distillation is the commonest method of extracting oils. Plant material is put into a still and steamed under pressure. The heat and steam encourage the essences which are in the specialised cells of the plant to be released and vaporised. The steam which contains the vaporised oil is then cooled in a condenser. The essential oil is insoluble in water. Dependent upon its density it will either float or sink in the liquid thus allowing the essential oil to be removed. The by-product of distillation produces flower or herbal water (e.g. rose water; lavender water).

Expression is the method used to extract essential oils from the outer coloured rind of citrus fruits. The machine method of expression is used most frequently today.

Enfleurage is the method used to make the absolutes such as Rose,

Jasmine and Neroli. It is a labour intensive and lengthy process which partly accounts for the high cost of these oils.

Glass sheets are coated with fat, then freshly picked flower heads are sprinkled over the fat. The sheets are then stacked in tiers to allow the essence in the flower head to be absorbed into the fat. They are left for several days, then, the old dead flower heads are removed and replenished with fresh ones. This process can take up to three months for the fat to become completely saturated with the essence of the flowers. The fat will then be collected and cleaned of debris. At this stage it is called a pomade. The pomade is dissolved in alcohol and the fat is filtered out to separate it from the absolute.

Choosing your essential oils

When choosing essential oils, use the following guidelines to ensure that you have high quality pure essential oils which are suitable for therapeutic use.

Essential oils are generally sold in 10 ml bottles, but you can find some smaller sizes.

Purchase oils from a reputable source.

Always buy essential oils that are sold in dark glass bottles, oils in clear glass bottles are not likely to be pure essential oils.

Sunlight can cause deterioration of essential oils, so make sure the oils are not sitting on a shelf exposed to direct sunlight. Store in a dark cool place.

The label should refer to the botanical name in addition to the name of the oil and the term PURE ESSENTIAL OIL.

A pipette inserted in the neck of the bottle, or a dropper insert, will allow for easy and correct measurement of drops.

Essential oils should not be stored in plastic bottles, as some of the chemicals in the plastic can interact with the essential oil constituents, damaging the container and spoiling the oil.

'Aromatherapy oils' are not pure essential oils; many of these mixed blends are sold in stores and supermarkets; they may have a pleasant smell but they are not for therapeutic use so cannot be used for clinical purposes. I have known people experience an unpleasant skin reaction following the use of some of these so called "aromatherapy oils". They may be fragrant but they are not therapeutic. Synthetic lotions and creams are not compatible with pure essential oils. They will interfere with the therapeutic properties of the oils and negate their use.

Prices of essential oils vary according to their scarcity or the labour involved in distillation. Be wary of oils that are all the same price, these are unlikely to be pure essential oils.

Some essential oils are extremely potent and can be highly toxic.

Oils not to be used at all in aromatherapy

Arnica, Bitter Almond, Boldo leaf, Calamus, Camphor Brown, Camphor Yellow, Bitter Fennel, Horseradish, Jaborandi Leaf, Mugwort, Mustard, Pennyroyal, Rue, Sage (common), Sassafras, Savine, Tansy, Thuja, Wormwood, Wormseed, Wintergreen.

If you find any oils not listed in this book avoid purchasing them until you have found reliable information concerning their safety.

Caring for your essential oils

Essential oils once opened will last for 18 to 24 months. Unopened, and correctly stored, they are safe and effective to use for up to about three years.

Always store the bottles in a cool dark place, away from direct heat and sunlight.

Replace the cap as soon as you have finished using the oil. Oils are volatile and will evaporate if left uncovered.

Citrus oils do not keep as well as other oils. Once opened, six months is the limit of their therapeutic usage.

Even water contaminates an essential oil.

Your carrier oils such as sweet almond oil, grapeseed oil, etc. should be used within three to four months. Do not be tempted to hoard.

Once you have blended an essential oil with a carrier oil potency is limited to about 12 weeks. After this the therapeutic properties will deteriorate and cannot be guaranteed to be effective. Blend small amounts that you will use within 12 weeks.

Wheatgerm oil is a natural anti-oxidant which can be added to a blend to extend its shelf life. A few drops are all that are required.

Keep the oils in a tin or invest in a custom made essential oil box, this will last a lifetime.

Carrier oils

These are unperfumed vegetable oils, which should be of the highest quality. They are used to dilute the essential oils for massage purposes.

Grapeseed Oil is a very commonly used, easily absorbed, light, carrier oil.

Sweet Almond Oil is extracted from the almond kernel; it is slightly lighter than grapeseed oil and easily absorbed. It contains vitamins A, B1, B6 and a small amount of vitamin E.

Jojoba Oil is a light golden oil particularly suitable for the face.

Evening Primrose Oil is particularly effective for massage when treating any disorder associated with hormonal imbalance. Use it as a 25% dilution in conjunction with another carrier oil.

Peach Kernel Oil contains minerals; it is light and easily absorbed, and therefore particularly good for facial use.

Avocado Oil is a dark green coloured oil particularly good for dry, ageing skin and arthritic conditions. Use as a 25% dilution with another carrier oil.

Wheatgerm Oil has a dark orange colour and is rich in vitamin E. It can act as an antioxidant when mixed with other carrier oils thereby prolonging the life and therapeutic use of the mixed oils. It is particularly good in helping to heal scar tissue.

Essential Oil Notes

Essential oils have a Top, Middle or Base Note.

The Top notes are light, stimulating and classed as body energising and uplifting; they also float on top of water.

The Middle notes are levelling, balancing and calming; they are partly soluble in water.

The Base notes are calming, sedative and relaxing; these sink to the bottom in water.

Essential oils are soluble in vegetable oil.

To achieve the perfect mix a top, middle and base note oil should be included in your blend.

For example, when treating some of the symptoms of pre-menstrual tension.

Breast Tenderness due to fluid retention:

	Top	Lemon	3 drops
Headache:	Middle	Lavender	4 drops
Aching muscles:	Base	Ginger	3 drops

Blending these essential oils with 20mls of a carrier oil and then massaging into the face, back, lower abdomen and legs will give considerable relief. The lemon is a mild diuretic, lavender is relaxing and analgesic, and ginger will stimulate the circulation and ease muscular aches and pains. The synergistic blend of oils are effective for the whole body.

PROPERTIES OF ESSENTIAL OILS

ANALGESIC
Relief of pain: Lavender, Chamomile, Rosemary, Ginger, Marjoram

ANTI-INFLAMMATORY
Reduces inflammation: Chamomile, Lavender, Myrrh, Bergamot

ANTISEPTIC
Combats bacterial infection locally: Lavender, Bergamot, Eucalyptus, Tea Tree, Lemon

ASTRINGENT
Tightens the tissues, helps to reduce fluid loss: Lemon, Cypress, Sandalwood, Myrrh

ANTISPASMODIC
Helps to reduce muscle spasm: Chamomile, Lavender, Ginger

ANTIDEPRESSANT
Has an uplifting effect on the nervous system: Bergamot, Geranium, Orange, Petitgrain

ANTI-VIRAL
Aids in combating a virus: Tea Tree, Lemon, Lavender

BACTERICIDAL
Helps to kill bacteria: Eucalyptus, Lemon, Lavender, Rosemary, Tea Tree, Bergamot

BACTERIOSTATIC
Helps to inhibit the growth of bacteria: Lavender, Tea Tree, Lemon, Eucalyptus, Bergamot

CEPHALIC
Stimulates mental activity: Peppermint, Rosemary

CHOLAGOGUE
Stimulates bile flow: Lavender, Rosemary, Chamomile

CYTOPHYLACTIC
Aids in cell regeneration: Lavender, Tea Tree, Neroli

CARMINATIVE
Reduces intestinal spasm: Ginger, Lavender, Peppermint, Chamomile, Rosemary, Orange

DEODORANT
Reduces odour: Lemongrass, Cypress, Petitgrain, Rosemary

DETOXIFYING
Stimulates excretion of waste products from the body: Juniper, Lemon, Fennel

DECONGESTANT
Relieves congestion: Eucalyptus, Rosemary, Benzoin

DIURETIC
Increases the output of urine: Bergamot, Chamomile, Cypress, Fennel, Juniper, Lavender

11

EMMENAGOGUE	*Encourages menstruation:* Lavender, Chamomile, Marjoram, Juniper, Clary Sage, Rosemary, Rose, Jasmine, Basil, Myrrh
EXPECTORANT	*Helps to expel phlegm:* Eucalyptus, Benzoin, Sandalwood, Bergamot
FEBRIFUGE	*Helps to reduce a fever:* Bergamot, Peppermint, Eucalyptus, Lavender
FUNGICIDAL	*Inhibits the growth of fungi yeasts:* Tea Tree, Myrrh, Lavender
HEPATIC	*Assists the liver:* Chamomile, Cypress, Lemon
HYPERTENSIVE	*Raises the blood pressure:* Rosemary
HYPNOTIC	*Helps to induce sleep:* Lavender, Marjoram, Chamomile
HYPOTENSIVE	*Helps to lower a raised blood pressure:* Lavender, Marjoram, Ylang Ylang
IMMUNO-STIMULANT	*Helps to strengthen the immune response to infection:* Lavender, Tea Tree, Lemon
NERVINE	*Helps to strengthen the nervous system:* Chamomile, Lavender, Rosemary, Marjoram
RELAXANT	*Aids mental relaxation:* Chamomile, Clary Sage, Lavender, Marjoram, Ylang Ylang
RUBEFACIENT	*Produces a warming effect when applied to the skin:* Black Pepper, Ginger, Benzoin, Eucalyptus, Juniper
SEDATIVE	*Has a calming effect on the nervous system:* Chamomile, Clary Sage, Frankincense, Lavender, Marjoram, Rose
STIMULANT	*Has a stimulating effect on the whole body:* Eucalyptus, Geranium, Rosemary, Peppermint
UTERINE	*Has a tonic effect on the uterus:* Clary Sage, Rose, Jasmine
VASOCONSTRICTOR	*Causes contraction of capillaries:* Chamomile, Cypress, Lemon, Rose
VASODILATOR	*Causes expansion of capillaries:* Marjoram
VULNERARY	*Will aid in the healing of wounds:* Benzoin, Bergamot, Lemon, Eucalyptus, Tea Tree, Lavender, Myrrh

Now to their use

Massage: In aromatherapy massage the essential oils are added to a carrier oil such as sweet almond oil before applying to the skin. Massage is one of the best ways of using oils as it can help to relax the body, reduce muscular tension, stimulate the circulation and the immune system, help to reduce stress and anxiety and promote a feeling of well-being.

Aromatic Baths: These are an excellent way of relieving aches and pains due to menstrual cramp. Depending upon the choice of essential oil, the bath can be relaxing to aid restful sleep or invigorating and stimulating or soothing to give relief from muscular aches and pains.

Sitz Baths or shallow baths: These are ideal for bathing the genital area when a woman is suffering with haemorrhoids or a urinary tract infection.

Foot Baths: These provide relief for aching feet and stimulate circulation for those who suffer with cold feet. Foot baths with the addition of anti-fungal oils are helpful in the treatment of conditions such as athlete's foot.

Lotions and Creams: These must be pure vegetable based and unscented; they are a good media in which to dilute essential oils for your face and body:

LOTIONS

Recommended concentration for adults is a $2\frac{1}{2}$% dilution.

Example: 100 mls of unscented lotion to which add 50 drops of essential oils.

Shake well into the lotion to ensure it is well mixed.

People with sensitive skin should use a $1\frac{1}{4}$% dilution.

Example: 100 mls unscented lotion to which add 25 drops of essential oils.

CREAMS

These should be pure vegetable based and unperfumed.

The recommended concentration is $1\frac{1}{4}$% dilution.

Example: 60 mls unscented cream to which add 15 drops of essential oil. For a sensitive skin add 7 drops to 60 mls of cream.

Showers: Add essential oils to a base shower gel then use on a loofah. This will give a lovely invigorating shower.

Shampoos: Add essential oils to a base unscented shampoo. The choice of essential oils will depend upon hair and scalp condition. For example Rosemary oil will stimulate the scalp. Chamomile Roman helps to relieve a dry itchy scalp. Tea Tree is beneficial where there is dandruff. The recommended concentration is a 1% dilution.

Example: 100 mls of base shampoo to which add 25 drops of essential oils.

Steam inhalations: Add essential oils to a bowl of steaming hot water, place a towel over the head and inhale the vapours. Steam inhalations are beneficial for treating a sore throat, cleansing the skin and decongesting blocked sinuses.

Vaporisation in a burner: Vaporisation of essential oils is an important therapeutic use of essential oils. Depending upon the choice of oils used, the molecules which are vaporised can have either a calming relaxing effect, or stimulate, aiding concentration. Many of the oils used to vaporise can help to kill airborne bacteria and are an effective weapon against infection.

To vaporise an oil: Fill the vessel with hot water. Add 6 drops of essential oil to the water. Place a night light in the base of the burner, this will keep the water hot thus allowing vaporisation.

Water sprays: A spray bottle filled with natural spring water can have essential oils added. It can then be used as a skin freshener, or in a room or car as an air freshener.

Compress: A compress is excellent for the relief of menstrual cramp and is effective for people who cannot get into a bath. The addition of analgesic and antispasmodic oils to a hot compress can help to relieve chronic pain.

For a hot compress, fill a bowl with 2 pints of very hot water. Add up to 6 drops of essential oils. Immerse a clean flannel, wring out and apply to the area to be treated. Cover it with clingfilm and a dry towel, leave in place for 15 minutes. Remove and very gently massage the area to alleviate any congestion of blood. To make a cold compress the same principle applies using very cold water. (A cold compress is effective for acute pain such as a sprain).

Oils on a tissue or handkerchief: This is a quick and effective way of using an oil. One drop is generally all that is required. For example when one has a cold, Eucalyptus can help to decongest blocked sinuses.

Gargles: This is helpful in the treatment of a sore throat and mouth ulcers. Fill a tumbler with water, add one drop of Tea Tree essential oil, mix well. Gargle holding the mouthwash in the mouth for a few seconds at a time. Do this three times each day until the condition has cleared. Do not swallow.

Diluting and blending essential oils

The recommended concentration is $2\frac{1}{2}\%$ for adults.

Example: 100 mls of a carrier oil, or lotion, add 50 drops of oil to it.
100 mls carrier oil; add 50 drops
50 ml carrier oil; add 25 drops
30 ml carrier oil; add 15 drops
20 mls carrier oil; add 10 drops
Essential oils have a pipette or "dropper" for easy measuring. Up to three different essential oils can be blended together.

Children up to the age of eleven years, and adults with sensitive skin should use a $1\frac{1}{4}$% dilution.
Example: 100 mls add 25 drops
50 mls add 12 drops
30 mls add 7 drops
20 mls add 5 drops

During Pregnancy: $1\frac{1}{4}$% dilution.
Example: 100 mls add 25 drops
50 mls add 12 drops
30 mls add 7 drops
20 mls add 5 drops

Blending your essential oil with a carrier oil

Fill a dark glass bottle with the amount you need. Select your essential oils; calculate the number of drops you need and add them to the bottle of carrier oil. Screw the dropper cap firmly; shake well to blend. Label and date the bottle ready for use.

2 | Essential oils for women's health – how to use the oils

BASIL ~
Ocimum basilicum

Uses: Breast Engorgement, Menstrual Cramps, Mental Fatigue, Influenza, Respiratory infections, Gastric colic.

Caution: Avoid using during pregnancy. Can be a skin irritant. Best administered under the guidance of a qualified aromatherapist.

Basil is a stimulating and tonic essential oil. It has antispasmodic properties which can be of help with menstrual conditions. It is also a nervine tonic.

Methods of use: Baths, Creams, Lotions, Compress, Massage and Vaporisation.

BENZOIN ~
Styrax benzoin

Uses: Coughs, Colds and Sore Throats, Dry cracked skin, Nervous tension.

Benzoin is an excellent antiseptic for use where there is infection of the respiratory tract. It is very effective when used as an inhalation to help expel thick mucous so relieving respiratory congestion.

Methods of use: Baths, Creams, Lotions, Compress, Massage and Vaporisation.

BERGAMOT ~
Citrus bergamia

Uses: Cystitis, Leucorrhoea, Thrush, Anxiety and Stress, General skin care, Vaginal Pruritis.

Caution: Can be a skin irritant. Avoid sunbathing or the use of sunbeds following its application. Always use diluted.

Bergamot is particularly effective for conditions of the genito-urinary system such as cystitis, thrush and urethritis. It has analgesic, antiseptic and anti-fungal properties. It is also helpful for treating infected skin conditions (such as acne, which can be troublesome at puberty) as it helps to balance the sebum level of the skin. Bergamot can be helpful during the menopause when there is mood disturbance due to hormonal imbalance.

Methods of use: Baths, Creams, Lotions, Compress, Shampoos, Massage and Vaporisation.

BLACK PEPPER ~
Piper nigrum

Uses: Poor circulation, Constipation, Muscular aches and pains, Digestive upsets.

Caution: Can be a skin irritant.

Black pepper used in very low dosage can be a valuable oil where stimulating and warming effects are required, for example in the treatment of muscular aches and pains or menstrual cramps.

For these conditions use it in a massage blend or in a compress.

Methods of use: Creams, Lotions, Compress, Massage.

CEDARWOOD ATLAS ~
Cedrus atlantica

Uses: Cystitis, Respiratory tract infections, Anxiety and Stress, Vaginal infections.

Caution: Avoid using during pregnancy.

Cedarwood is a very effective antiseptic and can be beneficial in the treatment of respiratory and urinary tract infections. It is helpful where there are skin infections such as spots, boils and acne. It is also a sedative essential oil for nervousness.

Methods of use: Baths, Creams, Lotions, Compress, Massage and Vaporisation.

CLARY SAGE ~
Salvia sclarea

Uses: Dysmenorrhoea, Labour Pains, Leucorrhoea, Emotional exhaustion.

Caution: Avoid using during pregnancy. Avoid alcohol as the combination of the two could precipitate fitful sleep.

Clary Sage should always be used in low dosage as it can cause euphoria, leaving the user feeling very light headed. Avoid driving after the use of this oil.

Clary Sage can help to regulate hormonal imbalance because it contains plant hormones similar to oestrogen. It is therefore invaluable for Pre-menstrual Tension and Menopausal problems. Clary Sage is a strong muscle relaxant. When used in a compress placed on the lower abdomen following birth, it can help to expel the placenta. Used in a massage blend

over the lower back it will help to alleviate menstrual cramps.
It is of immense value as a powerful anti-depressant.
Methods of use: Baths, Creams, Lotions, Compress, Massage and Vaporisation.

CHAMOMILE ROMAN ~
Anthemis Nobilis
Uses: Dysmenorrhoea, Menopausal problems, Menorrhagia, Cystitis, Anxiety, Insomnia, Stress, Dry Itchy Scalp, Swollen painful joints.
Caution: Avoid the use of Chamomile for the first 12 weeks of pregnancy. Any history of bleeding or of miscarriage do not use.
Chamomile Roman is analgesic, antispasmodic and a nerve sedative. This makes it a particularly useful essential oil for problems related to the menstrual cycle, or in any condition where there is muscular spasm. It also has a vaso-constricting effect on the capillaries when diluted and applied locally to the skin. This helps to make it an excellent anti-inflammatory oil. A 1% dilution in an unscented vegetable based lotion, gently applied to dry eczema will give considerable relief from itching and irritation. Chamomile is also a mild diuretic so will help to reduce fluid retention due to hormonal imbalance.
Methods of use: Baths, Creams, Lotions, Compress, Shampoos, Massage and Vaporisation.

CYPRESS ~
Cupressus sempervirens
Uses: Dysmenorrhoea, Menopausal problems, Menorrhagia, Cystitis, Haemorrhoids, Varicose Veins, Nervous Tension.
Cypress can be helpful in regulating the menstrual cycle. It has an astringent effect which causes a constricting effect on capillaries making it useful in the treatment of haemorrhoids and varicose veins. In these circumstances six drops of cypress added to a warm bath will help. The antispasmodic action of cypress will aid in the control of an asthma attack. In these circumstances do not vaporise the oil, use one drop on a tissue and gently inhale periodically. This oil is antiseptic and therefore beneficial in the treatment of urinary tract infections.
    For the relief of dysmenorrhoea use cypress in the bath, massage blends and in a compress.
Methods of use: Baths, Creams, Lotions, Compress, Massage and Vaporisation.

FENNEL ~
Foeniculum vulgare
Uses: Cellulite, Dysmenorrhoea, Pre-menstrual Tension, Menopausal

symptoms, Constipation, Nervous anxiety, Indigestion.

Caution: Avoid using during pregnancy, and do not use on children under six years as it contains a constituent (melanthine) which could prove harmful to them. Anyone suffering with epilepsy should also avoid the use of Fennel.

Fennel is a good detoxifying essential oil. It has diuretic properties and for this reason it should be used with caution and ideally under the supervision of an aromatherapist. Fennel is effective for conditions of the menstrual cycle. It is thought to contain a plant hormone which is similar in action to oestrogen which helps to regularise the menstrual cycle. Its antispasmodic effect helps to relieve menstrual cramps. Fennel can help to strengthen peristalsis of the large intestine and so is useful for adults who suffer from constipation. It has a carminative action so will give rapid relief from indigestion and digestive upsets when used in a massage blend and gently massaged over the abdomen.

Methods of use: Baths, Creams, Lotions, Compress, Massage and Vaporisation.

FRANKINCENSE ~
Boswellia carteri

Uses: Cystitis, Dysmenorrhoea, Leucorrhoea, Skin care, Heavy periods, Nervous Tension and Anxiety.

Frankincense is a uterine tonic thus beneficial for those who suffer with heavy periods. It is also an oil which is particularly good for dry mature skin.

As a result of its antifungal, antiseptic and anti-inflammatory properties it has been found to be of great help in treating conditions where there is infection of the genito-urinary system.

Vaporised it has a profoundly calming effect thus helping to allay anxiety and tension.

Methods of use: Baths, Creams, Lotions, Compress, Massage and Vaporisation.

EUCALYPTUS ~
Eucalyptus globulus

Uses: Sinusitis, Respiratory Tract infections, Urinary Tract infections, Muscular aches and pains, Leucorrhoea, Hay Fever.

Eucalyptus is a strong antiseptic with bactericidal properties. It can be used effectively to help treat bacterial and viral infections of the respiratory and urinary tract. It is an excellent decongestant oil that can help to relieve sinusitis and catarrh. It has a warming effect when applied to the skin through massage, in a lotion or a compress, thus helping to relieve muscular aches and pains.

Methods of use: Baths, Creams, Lotions, Compress, Massage and Vaporisation.

GERANIUM ~
Pelargonium graveolens

Uses: Cellulite, Engorged Breasts, menopausal symptoms, Pre-menstrual Tension, Nervous Tension, General skin care.

Caution: Avoid the use of Geranium for the first 12 weeks of pregnancy. Any history of bleeding or miscarriage do not use.

Geranium is an adrenal cortex stimulant. This oil is helpful in dealing with menopausal problems and pre-menstrual tension when there is hormonal imbalance. The diuretic action of Geranium is effective in the treatment of cellulite. During PMT, if there are erratic mood swings, vaporising geranium can help to balance and calm the feelings of anxiety and irritability which can occur a few days prior to menstruation.

Geranium can have a stimulating effect on the lymphatic system and is therefore beneficial when used in a massage blend in the treatment of cellulite, and fluid retention.

Methods of use: Baths, Creams, Lotions, Compress, Shampoos, Massage and Vaporisation.

GRAPEFRUIT ~
Citrus paradisi

Uses: Fluid retention, Acne, Mental fatigue, Skin and hair care.

Grapefruit is a wonderful uplifting and stimulating oil with strong antiseptic properties.

It has a mild diuretic effect and so can be helpful in the relief of fluid retention due to hormonal imbalance.

It is beneficial in the treatment of greasy skin.

Methods of use: Baths, Creams, Lotions, Compress, Shampoo, Massage and Vaporisation.

GINGER ~
Zingiber officinale

Uses: Digestive upsets, Nausea, Menstrual Cramps, Rheumatic aches and pains, Nervous exhaustion.

Caution: Possible skin irritant.

Ginger has a carminative effect on the digestive system so can help to quell nausea and give relief from gastric colic. Due to its strong antispasmodic action it is effectively used in a massage blend or a compress for the relief of period pains. It is a good circulatory tonic and very effectively used in the treatment of muscular aches and pains for those who suffer with cold feet due to poor circulation.

Methods of use: Baths, Creams, Lotions, Compress, Massage and Vaporisation.

JASMINE ~
Jasminum officinale

Uses: Dysmenorrhoea, Labour pains, Depression, Anxiety, General skin care.

Caution: Avoid using during pregnancy.

Jasmine is a uterine tonic. It can be used to relieve menstrual cramps. During the first and second stages of labour, when used in a massage blend over the lower back, it can help with pain relief. It is uplifting and calming on the emotions and therefore useful in a post natal capacity.

Methods of use: Baths, Creams, Lotions, Compress, Massage and Vaporisation.

JUNIPER ~
Juniperus communis

Uses: Cellulite, Cystitis, Leucorrhoea, Haemorrhoids, Dysmenorrhoea, Nervous tension and Anxiety, Fluid retention.

Caution: Avoid using during pregnancy. Avoid using on a person who has kidney disease.

Juniper is an excellent antiseptic and diuretic essential oil, therefore invaluable when the aim is to cleanse the body of accumulated toxins. It has a tonic effect on the genito-urinary systems and will aid in the treatment of disorders of these body systems. In the treatment of any urino-genital infection it is always advisable to seek the opinion of your doctor. Aromatherapy can complement and assist any medical treatment.

Methods of use: Baths, Creams, Lotions, Compress, Massage and Vaporisation.

LAVENDER ~
Lavendula angustifolia

Uses: Headaches, Menopausal problems, Pre-menstrual Tension, Dysmenorrhoea, Cystitis, Labour Pains, Anxiety, Insomnia, Stress, Hysteria.

Caution: Avoid using during the first twelve weeks of pregnancy.

Lavender is by far the most valuable and widely used essential oil. It has a balancing and regulating effect on both mind and body and can be blended with the majority of essential oils.

It has strong antiseptic, analgesic, antispasmodic and anti-inflammatory properties which make it beneficial in the treatment of many women's ailments. A useful tip for the treatment of minor burns and scalds; apply a few drops of neat lavender oil to the affected area to give relief from pain and aid in healing. To help aleviate anxiety and aid restful sleep, vaporise Lavender.

Methods of use: Baths, Creams, Lotions, Compress, Massage and Vaporisation.

LEMON ~
Citrus limonum

Uses: Cellulite, Haemorrhoids, Varicose veins, Mouth ulcers, General skin care, Verrucas, Warts, Mental Sluggishness.

Caution: Can be a skin irritant.

Lemon is a strong antiseptic and bactericidal oil. It is particularly effective in the treatment of varicose veins and haemorrhoids due to the astringent effect on the veins which aids in toning and tightening the tissue thus helping to prevent fluid loss.

Methods of use: Baths, Creams, Lotions, Compress, Massage and Vaporisation.

LEMONGRASS ~
Cymbopogon citratus

Uses: Athlete's foot, Excessive perspiration, Indigestion, Insect repellent, Panic attacks, Nervous tension.

Caution: Can be a skin irritant.

Lemongrass when used in a massage blend can be a tonic to the whole system. It is of particular value when used in the treatment of infectious illness and fevers. When vaporised it acts as an effective insect repellent.

Methods of use: Baths, Massage, Lotion, Creams and Vaporisation.

MARJORAM ~
Origanum marjorana

Uses: Pre-menstrual Tension, Dysmenorrhoea, Arthritis, Muscular aches and pains, Insomnia, Poor circulation, Nervous Tension.

Caution: Avoid using during pregnancy.

Marjoram with its warming effect and antispasmodic action is soothing and helps relieve menstrual cramps, arthritis and muscular aches and pains. In cases where insomnia and stress related conditions are present, vaporising marjoram can help to reduce anxiety and promote restful sleep.

Methods of use: Baths, Creams, Lotions, Compress, Massage and Vaporisation.

MANDARIN ~
Citrus nobilis

Uses: Fluid retention, Dyspepsia, Insomnia, Skin care.

Mandarin is carminative in its action and will quickly give relief from digestive upsets when blended in a carrier oil and gently massaged over the abdomen. This massage blend can also help in the prevention of stretch marks. It is one of the safest oils to use for children and during pregnancy.

Methods of use: Baths, Creams, Lotions, Compress, Massage and Vaporisation.

ORANGE ~
Citrus sinensis

Uses: Constipation, Cellulite, Digestive problems, Anxiety.

Caution: Can be a skin irritant. Use in low dosage.

Orange can be used in a massage blend to deal effectively with minor digestive upsets. Massage the blend gently over the abdomen. Orange oil is antiseptic and can be used for general skin care and in the treatment of acne and spots. When vaporised it has an uplifting and calming effect.

Methods of use: Baths, Creams, Lotions, Compress, Massage and Vaporisation.

NEROLI (Orange Blossom) ~
Citrus vulgaris

Uses: Diarrhoea, Colic, Muscular spasms, Flatulence, Skin care, Anxiety, Stress, Insomnia and Shock.

Neroli is excellent for skin care as it helps to stimulate the growth of healthy new cells. It is also a powerful antispasmodic which will help relieve spasm in the smooth muscle of the intestines. It can help with digestive disorders such as flatulence, indigestion and chronic diarrhoea. For these complaints use in a massage blend and gently massage over the abdomen. This oil has a calming effect on the central nervous system. It is effective when vaporised or used as one drop on a tissue which is then inhaled, this can be helpful when a person has just received a shock.

Methods of use: Baths, Creams, Lotions, Shampoos, Massage and Vaporisation.

NIAOULI ~
Melaleuca viridiflora

Uses: Boils, Acne, Insect bites, Cystitis, Sore throat, Catarrhal conditions, Thrush.

Niaouli is a strong antiseptic and fungicidal oil. It can be used to treat respiratory and urinary tract infections. It is non-irritant on the skin and therefore blended into an unperfumed lotion is effective in treatment of acne.

Methods of use: Baths, Creams, Lotions, Compress, Massage and Vaporisation.

MYRRH ~
Commiphora myrrha

Uses: Fungal skin conditions, Leucorrhoea, Vaginal Pruritis, Thrush, Insomnia.

Caution: Avoid using during pregnancy.

Myrrh is an antiseptic and fungicidal oil and is, therefore, helpful in the treatment of fungal infections of the genito-urinary system and the skin. It also has a tonic effect on the uterus.

Used in a cream it can aid in the healing of dry cracked skin of the hands and feet.

Methods of use: Baths, Creams, Lotions, Compress, Massage and Vaporisation.

PEPPERMINT ~
Mentha piperita

Uses: Flatulence, Indigestion, Digestive colic, Headaches, Mental fatigue, Nausea.

Caution: Avoid using during pregnancy. Can be a skin irritant.

This is a very strong oil and may counteract the effect of homeopathic remedies. Use with caution.

Peppermint is very effective in the relief of digestive upsets. It is both carminative and antispasmodic on the digestive system. One drop on a cold compress placed on the forehead can give relief from a headache.

This is very effective for feverish conditions. It is a cephalic stimulant and when vaporised can aid concentration.

Methods of use: Creams, Lotions, Compress, Massage, and Vaporisation.

PALMAROSA ~
Cymbopogon martini

Uses: Minor skin infections, Intestinal infections and Nervous Exhaustion.

Palmarosa can help to stimulate the production of healthy new skin cells. Due to its antiseptic and sebum balancing properties it is a valuable oil in the care of the skin.

Methods of use: Baths, Creams, Lotions, Compress, Massage and Vaporisation.

PETITGRAIN ~
Citrus bigaradia

Uses: Dyspepsia, Flatulence, Greasy skin and hair, Nervous exhaustion.

Petitgrain is a good digestive tonic. When incorporated in a massage blend and gently massaged over the abdomen in a clockwise direction, it will give relief from dyspepsia, trapped wind and indigestion. It is an uplifting oil and can be helpful in the treatment of depression.

Methods of use: Baths, Creams, Lotions, Compress, Massage and Vaporisation.

PATCHOULI ~
Pogostemon cablin

Uses: Athlete's foot, Skin care, Fungal infections, Nervous Exhaustion.

Patchouli is a very strong and overpowering scented essential oil which you either love or hate. It is particularly helpful in the treatment of fungal infections and in general skin care.

Methods of use: Baths, Creams, Lotions, Compress, Massage and Vaporisation.

ROSE ~
Rosa centifolia

Uses: Irregular Menstruation, Leucorrhoea, Uterine Disorders, General skin care, Insomnia, Frigidity, Stress.

Caution: Avoid using in massage blends during pregnancy for the first 12 weeks. If there is any history of bleeding or miscarriage do not use at all.

Rose centafolia is cleansing, regulating and tonic in its effect on the uterus. It is an excellent essential oil to use to complement the treatment of any gynaecological condition. On an emotional level it is of great benefit to women suffering from anxiety linked to problems of the reproductive system. In treatment for infertility and post-natal depression vaporising Rose will help to alleviate anxiety and nervous tension.

It is most helpful when there is dryness and sensitive facial skin as it can help to reduce inflammation.

Methods of use: Baths, Creams, Lotions, Compress, Massage and Vaporisation.

ROSEWOOD ~
Aniba rosaeodora

Uses: Coughs and colds, Nervous tension, Acne, Influenza.

Rosewood can be a beneficial essential oil as it has a general tonic effect on the whole body.

Methods of use: Baths, Creams, Lotions, Compress, Massage and Vaporisation.

ROSEMARY ~
Rosmarinus officinalis

Uses: Muscular aches and pains, Dysmenorrhoea, Respiratory Infections, and Mental lethargy, Asthma, Sinusitis, Influenza, Arthritis.

Caution: Avoid using during pregnancy.

Not to be used on anyone suffering with Epilepsy.

Rosemary is an invigorating and stimulating essential oil. It can help to relieve congestion and is therefore valuable in the treatment of fluid retention due to menstrual symptoms and cellulite.

As a mental tonic it aids concentration and promotes clarity of thought. It is highly antiseptic and analgesic which makes it a good choice when treating respiratory tract infections and muscular aches and pains. As it is an anti-spasmodic oil it is beneficial for the relief of menstrual cramps. It is a good circulatory oil, and tonic for the heart.

Methods of use: Baths, Creams, Lotions, Compress, Shampoos, Massage and Vaporisation.

SANDALWOOD ~
Santalum album

Uses: Urinary tract infections, Respiratory tract infections, Cystitis, Digestive disorders, Acne, Anxiety, Stress.

Sandalwood can be used in a massage blend and in the bath to help treat urinary tract infections. It is a pulmonary antiseptic so where there is excessive catarrh it can aid in cleansing and easing respiration. In these circumstances vaporise the oil and use it in a massage for the back and chest. Its antiseptic action can help to alleviate any troublesome spots and acne which can occur during puberty and sometimes during the menopause.

Methods of use: Baths, Creams, Lotions, Shampoos, Compress, Massage and Vaporisation.

TEA TREE ~
Melaleuca alternifolia

Uses: Thrush, Athlete's foot, Acne, Spots, Cystitis, Vaginitis, Vaginal Pruritis, Coughs and Colds, Cold sores, Warts, Veruccas and Dandruff.

Tea Tree oil is an exceptional antiseptic, bactericidal, antifungal and anti-viral oil. It can help to stimulate the immune system when it is under threat from infection. Tea Tree can be used neat dabbed onto a cold sore using a cotton bud. When there is a urinary tract infection, shallow cool baths with three drops of Tea Tree oil can be an effective treatment. These baths should be taken daily until the condition has cleared.

For mouth ulcers and gum infections prepare a Tea Tree gargle (as directed under 'How to Use Oils'; it is a highly effective treatment.

Methods of use: Baths, Creams, Lotions, Shampoos, Compress, Massage, Vaporisation and Gargle.

YLANG YLANG ~
Cananga odorata

Uses: Hypertension, Palpitations, Frigidity, Nervous Tension, Anxiety.

Caution: In concentrated amounts it can cause a headache.

Ylang Ylang has therapeutic properties which can help to calm anyone in an agitated state. In so doing it lowers raised blood pressure due to anxiety and tension. Those who may be suffering from sexual difficulties due to anxiety and stress have found the relaxing effect of Ylang Ylang highly beneficial.

Methods of use: Baths, Creams, Lotions, Shampoos, Massage and Vaporisation.

3 | Looking after your health with aromatherapy

Aromatherapy is your best friend when it comes to maintaining good health and coping with everyday life. Most women find themselves pulled in many directions; home; work; children; social activities, and sometimes care of elderly relatives.

All this consumes time and energy leaving many women too little time to themselves in which to re-charge the batteries and tone up the physique.

So look after yourself. This is not self indulgence for it can be a gift to your family and friends if all those feelings of irritability, anxiety and tension are dissolved away through relaxation.

Boosting immunity

By using essential oils on a regular basis you can defend yourself against a number of micro-organisms. Face and body lotions and vaporising oils in your home, working environment and baths can help to strengthen and boost the immune system. In this way your body resists opportunistic infections such as colds, influenza, sore throats and stress related conditions.

Vaporising essential oils such as Tea Tree, Rosemary, Lemon, Eucalyptus and Lavender can help to neutralise air-borne micro-organisms so creating a healthier home and working environment. The anti-bacterial effect of essential oils can be used more specifically, for instance Tea Tree may be used to clean the telephone mouthpiece which tends to harbour bacteria.

Aromatherapy for restful sleep

Use essential oils in your home to establish a regular sleeping pattern. Vaporise a calming gentle sedative oil such as Lavender or Chamomile during the evening. These oils can have a subtle relaxing effect and give your room a lovely aroma.

Avoid caffeine as much as possible and drink decaffeinated tea and coffee, mineral water, fruit juices or herbal teas.

Drink a cup of herbal tea containing gentle sedative herbs approximately one hour before retiring for the night. Examples of herbal sedatives include Passiflora, Valerian and Hops.

Each evening take a relaxing hot bath adding an essential oil of your choice.

Massage given by your partner will relax tension in the muscles and promote restful sleep.

Promoting good circulation

Help your circulatory system in order to provide vital nutrients and send oxygenated blood to all parts of the body. Massage stimulates lymph flow and aids the circulation of lymphocytes and other white cells around the body in the fight against infection.

Mandarin essential oil is a good lymphatic tonic.

Varicose veins are often associated with poor circulation and can develop into varicose ulcers in later life which are painful. When there is impaired circulation such ulcers may prove difficult to heal.

To help prevent varicose veins avoid standing for long periods.

When relaxing elevate your legs, this will help the return of venous blood to the heart.

Walk as much as possible and use stairs rather than lifts.

Massage your legs and feet daily with a blend of essential oils.

Massage blend:	Carrier oil	20 mls
	Add Marjoram	5 drops
	Ginger	5 drops

Always massage towards the heart.

Alternatively use a lotion on your legs and feet daily, the oils in the lotion below are good for the circulation.

Lotion	100 mls base lotion	
	Add Marjoram	20 drops
	Lavender	15 drops
	Ginger	15 drops

When bathing add 6 drops in total to your bath using any of the following essential oils: Marjoram, Ginger or Juniper.

If you already have varicose veins take baths with the addition of Cypress or Lemon essential oils. These oils are astringent in action and will help strengthen tissues and prevent fluid loss.

Do not massage over varicose veins.

Treat your varicose veins gently. Apply a lotion gently to your legs avoiding pressure over the veins. Start at the feet and work up your legs.

Lotion   100 mls
                Add   Cypress   25 drops
                      Lemon   25 drops

Helping to prevent cramps and chilblains

Practice the same routine as for prevention of varicose veins.

How essential oils help emotional balance

When vaporised, essential oils can be inhaled because the aromatic molecules are tiny enough to pass directly into the blood stream in the same way as oxygen. This can have a rapid effect.

The odours stimulate the nerve endings in the Olfactory Bulb which lies at the back of the nose. Here the nerve endings stimulate a part of the brain known as the Limbic System, a complex network of nerve endings associated with our emotions and memories.

The nerve endings in the Limbic system stimulate the Hypothalamus which controls the Pituitary Gland. This in turn controls the Endocrine System which is responsible for regulating body processes such as reactions to fear, anger, metabolism and sexual stimuli. Study the oils to enable you to make the correct choice for a particular need.

For example, Lavender will calm and help to reduce anxiety, whilst Rosemary is a Cephalic stimulant which will promote alertness and aid concentration.

Balancing your emotions

Stress

No one gets through life without anxiety and stress; the challenge is what one makes of it. Stress can be the spur to action or positive thought. Without it one can become smug, ineffective or lethargic. It is only when anxiety and stress get out of control, and becomes excessive, giving rise to physical symptoms that it can be detrimental to our health.

Chronic anxiety can be triggered by stressful events such as divorce, redundancy, financial problems or a move to a new area.

If you experience a rapid heart rate, palpitations – a feeling of pounding in the chest, muscle tension, insomnia, digestive discomforts, tearfulness, a feeling of despair and fear, or any number of these symptoms suffered at any given time, then you must take heed and act.

A professional aromatherapist can help you to recognise and learn how to cope with nervous tension through the use of essential oils and massage. Use the opportunity to discuss repressed fears. Self help treatments empower you to counteract negative fears and anxieties and promote inner strength and balance.

Select from the following essential oils; Lavender, Marjoram, Ylang Ylang, Chamomile, Geranium and Clary Sage for use in a vaporiser, bath, or for massage. Give yourself the luxury of scented bedlinen.

If you get a feeling of sudden panic, put a drop of lemongrass on a handkerchief and inhale. This will give you relief.

Depression
All of us have 'down days'. It is when the feeling of depression is prolonged that it can lead to a serious medical condition requiring treatment.

There are many types of depression, sometimes it is a logical reaction to particular events in life, at other times it can develop for no apparent reason. Aromatherapy can complement medical treatment.

If you are just feeling low in spirits, select from any of the following energising and uplifting essential oils; Bergamot, Grapefruit, Lemon, Orange and Geranium for use in a vaporiser, bath or for massage.

Anger and intolerance
This may stem from pre-menstrual or menopausal symptoms; whatever the cause, escape from your family and make for your calming essential oils.

Select from any of the following for use in vaporisers, baths and for massage: Geranium, Chamomile, Lavender, Clary Sage, Ylang Ylang and Cedarwood.

Indecisiveness
We all experience this periodically, when choices and decisions are difficult to make. Try Frankincense, it helps you to relax into deep and careful thought. Use it in the bath and vaporiser.

When suffering a negative emotional state the Flower Remedies are immensely helpful.

Skin care essentials
There are a wide and complex variety of skin disorders. Here we will discuss the changes that can occur to healthy skin throughout a womans life.

The skin cells are in a constant state of renewal, with new cells replacing the old ones. This process slows down as we get older.

There are times, due to hormonal changes, when there are fluctuations in the production of sebum, a fatty material produced by the sebaceous glands which prevents the skin from becoming dry. If the production of sebum becomes imbalanced (over or under production) it can lead to dry or greasy skin problems.

During puberty, and sometimes during the menopause, when there is a possibility of hormonal imbalance, may become overactive resulting in the formation of spots and blackheads. Conversely, as we age there is a tendency for the skin to become drier as the cell renewal process slows down.

Remember your skin, hair and nails give an indication of the way you look after your body. Maintaining healthy tissues is dependent upon adopting good habits and abandoning bad ones.

Good habits to adopt

Cleanse, Tone and Moisturise your skin daily with products containing pure essential oils.

Use a loofah when bathing/showering to exfoliate old skin cells, then apply a body lotion enriched with oils suitable for your skin type.

Drink up to six to eight glasses of water, herbal tea or fruit juice each day. This encourages the body to eliminate waste and keeps the skin, mucous membranes and joints moist and well lubricated.

Don't make exercise a punishment or an 'expensive workout', take every opportunity to walk, swim and dance. Use the stairs rather than the lift whenever you can. If you have a 'desk job', stand and stretch regularly, and remember to drink plenty of water.

Relax your body and mind at the end of each day by enjoying a leisurely aromatic bath.

Bad habits to abandon

"Do you 'snack' on biscuits, cakes, chocolates, sweets or crisps?"

Try a piece of fruit or a fruit drink instead.

Hunger pangs are less likely to occur if you have had a good filling breakfast.

Tea and coffee have become a solace for most of us. It is easy to say cut down on these, so I will just recommend that some of those cups of tea or coffee could be replaced with a drink which is kinder to the digestive system and less likely to interfere with sleep, if you are a poor sleeper.

As recent research indicates, a glass of wine a day may even have health benefits. However, excess alcohol is potentially damaging, undermining the bodies immune system and leaving it more vulnerable to virulent antagonists.

Avoid saturated fats as much as possible as these types of fats are known to lead to the formation of fatty deposits in the lining of the arteries. Instead use vegetable oils in cooking, and where possible in moderation.

Smoking tends to increase the ageing process of the skin and make it look sallow. (Also most women who smoke screw up their eyes, creating unnecessary lines, distinct from laughter lines.)

Ensure that your food shopping is selective and avoid 'junk foods'. Salt exacerbates fluid retention so try using herbs for seasoning.

Essential oil skin care

Indulge yourself. Pure essential oils are a wonderful luxurious gift from nature and when blended into lotions, creams and toners can provide us with the purest nourishment and care for the skin. Please remember when blending essential oils into creams and lotions they should be vegetable based. Such creams and lotions are usually cocoa butter, jojoba, and almond oil based and are readily available at good health stores. Ordinary cosmetics tend to be disproportionately expensive, given their ingredients, so try making your own:

Moisturising cream for dry/mature skin

60 mls cream		
Add	Rose absolute	5 drops
	Sandalwood	5 drops
	Lavender	5 drops

Moisturising cream for dry/sensitive skin

60 mls cream		
Add	Chamomile	5 drops
	Sandalwood	5 drops
	Lavender	5 drops

Cream for oily skin (for use when there is a tendency to develop spots)

60 mls cream		
Add	Bergamot	5 drops
	Rosemary	5 drops
	Lavender	5 drops

Or

60 mls cream		
Add	Geranium	5 drops
	Bergamot	5 drops
	Lavender	5 drops

Moisturising cream for normal or combination skin

60 mls cream		
Add	Lavender	5 drops
	Bergamot	7 drops

Moisturising lotion for oily skin (to help clear spots and prevent reoccurrence)

100 mls Base unscented lotion		
Add	Lavender	16 drops
	Bergamot	16 drops
	Rosemary	18 drops

Or

        100 mls lotion
        Add   Lavender   16 drops
              Geranium   16 drops
              Lemon   18 drops

Body lotion particularly suitable for dry skin
        100 mls lotion
        Add   Lavender   16 drops
              Sandalwood 18 drops
              Palmarosa   16 drops

Lotion suitable for all skin types
        100 mls lotion
        Add   Orange   16 drops
              Geranium   16 drops
              Lavender   18 drops

Toner for oily skin
        50 mls Witch Hazel
        50 mls Orange flower Water
        Add   Lavender   5 drops
              Geranium   5 drops
              Bergamot   5 drops

Toner for dry skin
        50 mls Rose Water
        50 mls Witch Hazel
        Add   Palmarosa   5 drops
              Sandalwood 5 drops
              Lavender   5 drops

Toner for all skin types
        50 mls Witch Hazel
        50 mls Rose Water
        Add   Lavender   8 drops
              Petitgrain 7 drops

Cellulite

If you suffer from Cellulite, take note of the advice given previously.

TREATMENT FOR CELLULITE
Brush your skin prior to bathing using a natural bristle brush, this will stimulate the circulation and the lymphatic flow thus encouraging the elimination of waste products from your body.

Start at the feet and work upwards using circular movements.

Use an essential oil in your bath such as Lemon, Juniper or Geranium. All of these are detoxifying and mild diuretic oils.

After bathing apply one of the following lotions to your body, which will encourage detoxification of waste matter.

Cellulite Busters 100 mls lotion

Add	Juniper	10 drops
	Lemon	20 drops
	Geranium	20 drops

100 mls lotion

Add	Rosemary	20 drops
	Lemon	15 drops
	Juniper	15 drops

4 | The female reproductive system

The Vagina is the passage which leads from the vulva to the uterus. Following puberty the lining of the vagina becomes thick and rich in glycogen, the walls are well lubricated and elastic. Following the menopause the level of oestrogen falls and the walls tend to become thin and often dry. The mucous which has kept the vagina lubricated throughout the pre-menopausal years decreases. This can sometimes lead to infections and soreness of the vagina.

The Uterus is a hollow pear shaped organ which lies in the pelvic girdle, supported by the muscles of the pelvic floor.

It is made up of two parts, the body and the cervix.

It is a strong muscular organ and during pregnancy it expands to allow the foetus to grow.

After birth the uterus quickly returns to its normal size.

The lining of the uterus is called the Endometrium and each month from puberty to menopause the endometrium will develop in preparation for a fertilised egg. If an egg is not fertilised then the lining will break down and is shed as the monthly blood flow.

The Fallopian Tubes are two tubes one on either side of the uterus. They are approximately 10cms in length. Their function is to propel the egg from the ovary into the cavity of the uterus.

The Ovaries are two small almond sized glands which lie one on either side of the uterus, held in place by strong elastic ligaments. They make and release eggs. By puberty they will contain approximately 40,000 to 400,000 eggs, of which only 500 eggs will ever by released. They begin to function at puberty and will continue to release an egg each menstrual cycle until the onset of menopause.

The ovaries function under the control of the pituitary gland.

The Menstrual Cycle

From the start of a period to the first day of the next is known as the menstrual cycle and takes between approximately 28 to 31 days. This can vary from one woman to another. The cycle is controlled by the hypothalamus in the brain, which operates via the anterior pituitary gland.

The hormones oestrogen and progesterone are produced by the ovaries and are stimulated by a hormone from the pituitary gland under the control of the hypothalamus. The hypothalamus can be affected by our emotions, therefore menstruation can be influenced and disturbed by worries, anxieties and stress.

Follicle stimulating hormone is released from the pituitary gland to the ovary. The hormone producing cells and the egg are together called the Graafian Follicle. This follicle produces oestrogen which allows the lining of the uterus to thicken, it also changes the secretions of the vagina which allows the sperm to swim with ease into the uterus to meet an egg.

This is known as the oestrogenic phase and lasts for approximately 14 days.

The second half of the cycle then begins, known as the progestogenic phase. The pituitary gland begins to secrete Luteinizing Hormone which stimulates an egg to be released from the ovary. This occurs within 24 to 36 hours.

This egg will travel down the fallopian tube into the uterus where it will await possible fertilisation with a sperm.

The cells from the Graafian Follicle now undergo changes and begin to fill up with a yellow substance. It is now known as the Corpus Luteum, and secretes oestrogen and progesterone.

The progesterone alters the consistency of the mucous at the neck of the uterus, the mucous becomes thick and sticky thus preventing sperm swimming through it. The progesterone also increases the blood supply and nourishment to the endometrium so that should fertilisation of an egg occur then the endometrium could sustain it.

The Corpus Luteum will secrete progesterone for approximately 14 days. If pregnancy does not occur then the levels of progesterone and oestrogen will fall and the lining of the uterus is shed, so begins the next menstrual cycle.

5 | Irregularities of menstruation

Irregular Periods

Firstly let us look at regular periods so that we know what is normal. The regularity of periods varies from one woman to another. Some women can have a period every twenty eight days whilst others may have a period every thirty to thirty five days, this is the usual pattern for most women.

Period patterns can be influenced by many circumstances such as changes in the seasons, bouts of dieting, travelling, stress, and changes in lifestyle. The regularity is determined by the interaction between the Hypothalamus, the Pituitary Gland, the Ovaries and the Uterus, as described in the workings of the menstrual cycle.

If your periods have altered in regularity take a look at any changes you have recently made in your life.

Aromatherapy can be of benefit in helping to regularise the menstrual cycle. Rose is not only a uterine tonic, it can have a calming effect on our emotions and help to balance body systems.

Lavender and Clary Sage are two oils which help to reduce anxiety.

Geranium is beneficial for hormonal imbalance.

Use these oils in massage blends, vaporisation and in baths regularly throughout the month.

For a menstrual cycle that has suddenly become irregular I would recommend aromatherapy massage. This will help to balance the body's energies and promote a calm and relaxed state of mind.

If the irregularity persists or there are other changes in the menstrual cycle such as bleeding between periods or prolonged heavy bleeding, then seek medical advice to ensure there is not an underlying medical condition that needs investigation.

Dysmenorrhoea (painful periods)

Many women suffer from menstrual cramps. They are often most severe on the first day of the period and are due to spasm of the uterus.

Dysmenorrhoea can be defined as:

Primary Dysmenorrhoea: menstrual cramp which is not caused by an underlying secondary organic pelvic disease.

Secondary Dysmenorrhoea: menstrual cramp caused by a pelvic disease such as Endometriosis or Fibroids.

In both cases aromatherapy treatments can help. There are many essential oils which have an antispasmodic effect on smooth muscle. These oils will ease the cramps caused by uterine spasm: Lavender, Chamomile Roman, Marjoram and Clary Sage are three such oils. These can be incorporated into a massage blend or lotion then gently massaged over the lower back and abdomen to help disperse the pain. Applying a hot compress (incorporating any of these oils) against the lower back and abdomen can also ease the discomfort.

Many of the essential oils which are antispasmodic are also emmenagogues. This means that they may also increase the menstrual flow.

Massage blends for Menstrual Cramps:

Carrier oil		20 mls
Add	Lavender	5 drops
	Marjoram	5 drops
Carrier oil		20 mls
Add	Chamomile Roman	3 drops
	Lavender	4 drops
	Marjoram	3 drops

BATHS: Add a total of six drops of any of the above essential oils to a hot bath then relax for at least 15 minutes.

Nutritional help

It has been found that certain nutritional supplements such as Evening Primrose oil (1000mgs per day) and Vitamin B6 taken in a B Complex tablet can be helpful in reducing menstrual cramps.

GLA – gamma linoleic acid, found in Evening Primrose Oil, helps your body to metabolise hormones correctly.

Chamomile tea is both sedative and a gentle antispasmodic.

Menorrhagia (heavy periods)

Although the period is regular each month, the menstrual flow can be of varying duration and flow. Every woman will have slightly different symptoms. If you suffer with heavy periods, which are regular, you may be able to use self help methods with success; whereas if the periods are heavy and irregular there could be an underlying disease which needs to be investigated by your doctor.

If your periods suddenly change and become heavy it could be due to any number of causes, for instance emotional strain.

Withdrawal from using the contraceptive pill may be followed by several months of heavy bleeding.

During the three to four years prior to the menopause women frequently experience heavier periods of short duration, or longer periods which are lighter in flow, or sometimes a combination of both.

The coil can be the cause of heavier periods.

There are also a number of more serious conditions which may change the menstrual flow.

Fibroids are non-cancerous tumours made up of muscle and fibrous tissue enclosed in a capsule and found in the uterus; some women can have several small fibroids at the same time which can cause painful and heavy periods; in some cases these can be the cause of irregular bleeding.

Endometriosis: The endometrium is the lining of the uterus which is shed during each monthly period if fertilisation does not occur. Endometriosis is another serious cause of irregular bleeding. This is a condition where the endometrium which normally lines the uterus, is found in abnormal places in the abdomen. The cause of endometriosis is not known. The symptoms can be variable from woman to woman. They include problems such as painful periods, backache, pelvic pain, irregular bleeding and heavy periods. Some women may have endometriosis and yet remain symptom free.

Aromatherapy and self help treatments for heavy periods.

Once you have satisfied yourself that your heavy periods are not due to any of the aforementioned serious conditions, you can then do a number of things which will help to alleviate the problem. In the case of heavy bleeding due to fibroids, these will tend to become smaller as the menopause approaches and oestrogen levels fall.

In the meantime try some of the self help treatments.

There are several essential oils which have a tonic and regulating effect on the reproductive organs: Rose, Clary Sage, Cypress, Geranium and Frankincense.

Aromatherapy massage can be given using a blend of any of these oils. The massage is effective given to the lower back and pelvic area. It is best done at midcycle. Such massage will increase energy flow to the pelvis.

Massage Blend:

	Carrier oil	30 mls
		Evening Primrose oil
Add	Geranium	8 drops
	Cypress	7 drops

Treat yourself to a professional aromatherapy massage about a week before your period is due, this will help release body energy, stimulate the circulation, and promote a feeling of well-being and relaxation.

Take a relaxing hot bath each evening with the addition of essential oils such as Lavender or Geranium. (Total of six drops)

Heavy periods can make a woman feel low in spirit, try vaporising any of the following essential oils for an uplifting and anti-depressant effect. Such oils are Mandarin, Bergamot, Lemon, Orange, Lemongrass and Petitgrain.

Remember that exercise tones up the whole system and raises the spirits.

Nutritional help

Eat plenty of iron rich foods such as: Liver, eggs, spinach, wheatgerm, and peanuts.

Vitamin C in fresh fruit and vegetables helps the body to absorb iron.

Avoid drinking stimulating drinks such as tea, coffee and cola.

Reduce your fat intake to a low fat and high fibre diet to gain considerable relief from your symptoms.

Evening Primrose Oil capsules taken as a nutritional supplement can sometimes help to normalise heavy periods.

Listen to your body

It is important to learn to listen to your body. If you are feeling tired and listless don't push yourself to do things that can wait. Instead do something that you enjoy, then take a long relaxing hot bath with some essential oils added to it. Have a cup of herbal tea containing a gentle sedative herb such as Chamomile to ensure a good night's rest.

Pre-menstrual Tension

This is commonly known as PMS or PMT, which many women suffer every month.

PMT symptoms are wide and varying and women can suffer from any number of them at any one time. Such symptoms cause great distress and disruption to personal and family happiness. The symptoms tend to come on gradually over a one to two week period prior to the onset of menstruation. They then stop abruptly when bleeding starts and it may feel as if a great emotional and physical burden has been lifted from the body.

Some women describe themselves as feeling out of control of their emotions for a two to three day period prior to the onset of menstruation.

Symptoms of Pre-menstrual Tension

Some women can show uncharacteristic moods of aggression, intolerance and impatience.

Concentration, on the other hand, can weaken and the woman can become weepy, depressed and easily upset.

Some women have co-ordination difficulties and feel that they are clumsy.

Some women experience tiredness, fatigue and lethargy.

As during pregnancy there can be food cravings especially for sweet or salty foods.

Migraine sufferers may find that their headaches can be triggered off by pre-menstrual tension.

The skin or hair can become greasy.

Coping with Pre-menstrual Tension

I always advise my clients suffering with PMT to keep a diary for three months. By keeping a note of how they feel each day during the fourteen days pre menstruation they are able to observe any negative patterns in symptoms. This can help towards planning, avoiding making important arrangements during the times which may be the most problematic, and developing a more opportunistic outlook.

Coping with Stress

Take a look at the Stress and pressures in your life. Try to identify what events or situations tend to make you feel more pressurised and endeavour to make the necessary changes.

If you go out to work, simple measures such as taking a relaxing bath on your return home and adding an essential oil such as Lavender, Orange, Bergamot or Geranium can do wonders. This pleasurable habit is also beneficial for busy mothers. Many find that three drops of Lavender in a child's bath ensures a good night's sleep for the child and a quiet one for mum.

Aromatherapy massage is excellent for any women who are suffering with PMT. The massage is most beneficial and effective a few days prior to menstruation as it will help to reduce anxiety, promote restful sleep, counteract lethargy and relieve a tension headache.

Such massage will stimulate the circulation and the lymphatic system so helping to relieve the fluid retention caused by hormonal imbalance. In severe cases of fluid retention I would recommend two massages during the second half of the menstrual cycle at weekly intervals.

The essential oils of choice for massage are:
Juniper for its detoxifying properties
Geranium as it stimulates the adrenal cortex and is associated with hormonal balance.
Rosemary as it is a circulatory stimulant.
Blend them with Evening Primrose oil as the carrier oil. (See dosage and blending)

Other helpful ways of using essential oils

VAPORISATION of essential oils.
Lavender helps promote calmness of the mind and restful sleep.
Bergamot or Mandarin have uplifting and anti-depressant properties.
Chamomile counteracts irritability.
Rosemary helps concentration.

AROMATIC BATHS containing Rosemary or Grapefruit restore depleted energy.
For relaxation add Lavender or Frankincense.
To aid restful sleep add Marjoram, Clary Sage or Lavender.

Following the bath use a body lotion with Geranium, Lavender and Rosemary essential oils added to it. These oils will help to tone and balance the body systems.

Lotion 100 mls unscented vegetable base lotion

	Add Lavender	17 drops
	Rosemary	16 drops
	Geranium	17 drops

Nutritional Help

Nutritional Help can give relief from many of the PMT symptoms and those of hormonal imbalance due to menopausal symptoms. The following information can therefore be applied in both instances.

Eliminate caffeine from the diet, this will be found in caffeinated teas, coffee and cola drinks. Cut out as much refined and processed foods as possible.

Reduce salt as sodium retains fluid and will therefore exacerbate fluid retention.

Cut down on sugars, an excessive amount of sugar gives the pancreas more work to do, more insulin is then required to metabolise the sugar. This is stressful to the body.

Eat a diet which is low in fat, this can help with hormonal balance.

Evening Primrose Oil can often help to alleviate PMT symptoms.

Reduce alcohol intake as this can exacerbate some of the symptoms.

Increase the intake of fresh fruit and vegetables.

Smoking can have a detrimental effect on the circulation and in many cases exacerbates some of the symptoms of PMT and those related to the menopause.

Gentle exercise: take a relaxing walk a couple of times each week for about twenty minutes, it is a good way to get away from everything.

Relaxation Techniques such as Yoga, Tai Chi and Meditation can have a profoundly relaxing effect on the whole body under the guidance of a skilled practitioner.

The herbal remedy Agnus Castus taken from midcycle until menstruation has been found by many women to help with the emotional effects that hormonal imbalance can cause. For menopausal symptoms Agnus Castus is usually recommended throughout the month.

THE MENOPAUSE

Most of you will understand what is happening during the menopause so I will briefly outline the stages of the climacteric so you can appreciate how aromatherapy can help.

Premenopause are years when the menstrual cycle is regular, or perhaps we should say approximately every 28 days since you may differ from the norm.

Peri-Menopause is a time when women become aware of physical changes. This stage can last several years with the onset varying from woman to woman. It usually starts in the early to mid-forties when the first symptoms are usually noticed in the menstrual cycle. The periods can become irregular, varying with each individual. For example menstruation can be as often as every twenty one days and with others it can be as long as eight to twelve weeks, then it might resume its normal monthly cycle for a period of time.

Menstrual flow can differ from one period to the next. The blood flow can be heavier for the first two days or it can be longer in duration but lighter in flow. Once again this is variable from one woman to another, there is no fixed pattern of change so do not worry if you seem to be different from the norm.

Menopause is marked by the last menstrual period the body ever has. Some women heave a sigh of relief; others view it pessimistically as an important phase of life over.

As a woman becomes menopausal there are changes in hormone secretion within her body. Regular menstruation created a normal balance of the hormones oestrogen and progesterone, changes will subsequently be noticed created by the hormonal imbalance and are thus reflected in various ways.

During the first two weeks of the cycle the oestrogen levels will fall as stimulation of egg follicles decrease. The supply of eggs in the ovaries is running out, therefore ovulation is less likely to occur. Without ovulation the corpus luteum is not produced, therefore progesterone is not secreted. This allows the oestrogen freedom to continue stimulating the growth of the uterine lining allowing it to continue to build up. When bleeding eventually occurs it will be heavier than normal and often contains clots of blood. The progesterone is required to oppose the effect of the oestrogen and prevent excessive thickening of the uterine lining.

When the ovaries finally cease to produce eggs, oestrogen and progesterone will no longer be secreted. This will lead to such low levels of oestrogen that stimulation of the lining of the uterus will not occur, then menstruation will stop.

Menopausal symptoms due to the effects of hormonal imbalance.

Women experiencing some of these symptoms for the first time can feel undue anxiety and tension, this in itself can exacerbate some of the symptoms.

Changes in body temperature can cause night sweats and hot flushes.

Mood changes such as anxiety, depression, and irritability may be experienced.

Skin changes such as dryness and itchiness may occur. (Women have described it to me as feeling as if little insects were crawling over their skin.)

Changes may take place in sleeping patterns causing for example, bouts of spasmodic insomnia.

Mental capacity can alter giving rise to poor concentration and forgetfulness.

Sexual drive can vary, some women have an increased libido whilst others lose sexual interest.

In the latter years lack of oestrogen can cause thinning of the vaginal walls; this results in dryness and itching creating discomfort during sexual intercourse.

Bladder weakness can follow the menopause creating an urgent need to pass urine.

Remember, however, that the great majority of women experience very few problems from the menopause. Keep a positive outlook and new challenges at this stage in your life will enhance your whole personality.

Now treat any or all of these symptoms

Night sweats and hot flushes

Again these vary in severity; some women awake drenched with perspiration and suffer from broken nights and chronic insomnia. This in turn leads to tiredness, causing irritability and sometimes depression.

Lavender essential oil is your life saver, a balm to the skin and the mind. Geranium and Rose essential oils help regulate hormonal imbalance. Rose has a very special function in being able to cleanse the uterus. Use both of these oils in massage, creams and lotions, baths and vaporisers on a regular basis.

45

Herbal remedies

Vitex agnus castus taken as a herbal tablet has been found by many women to help with menopausal symptoms caused by the imbalance of female hormones. It is particularly helpful for mood disturbance.

Siberian Ginseng root taken as a herbal tablet can help when there is a lack of energy.

Valerian taken in a herbal tablet or in an infusion of herbal tea is a well known and tried remedy for insomnia.

Poor concentration

Aim for better quality sleep. (See chapter on Promoting good health; Aids for restful sleep) When you wish to concentrate, vaporise essential oils such as peppermint or rosemary which are Cephalic stimulants.

Headaches

A few drops of neat Lavender oil massaged into the forehead and temples is effective for the relief of a headache.

Or apply a cold compress of 3 drops of lavender oil and one drop of peppermint.

Dry skin

Moisturise the skin daily with lotions and creams enriched with pure essential oils. (For some suggested blends see the chapter on Essential oil skin care)

Confidence

This can be weakened sometimes during and after the menopause. Rose, Jasmine, and Geranium are three very feminine essential oils. Pamper and indulge yourself with aromatherapy massage. It is important to value yourself and feel you are deserving of such care. Make this a regular habit as massage is beneficial for physical and mental well-being.

Vaginal dryness

This can be helped by using a simple carrier oil such as Evening Primrose Oil. Gently massage it into the vulva and vaginal area each night; this will also help to relieve painful intercourse caused by dryness of the vaginal walls.

Emotional ups and downs

I also recommend using the Flower Remedies.

Nutritional help

Please refer to this section under the chapter for Pre-menstrual Tension as many of the symptoms of hormonal imbalance can be relieved through dietary measures.

6 | Problems of the genito/urinary system

BARTHOLIN'S CYST

The Bartholins Glands are a pair of glands lying on each side of the opening to the vagina. In health we are unaware of their presence but if they become infected then a painful abscess can develop.

Aromatherapy treatment: Take warm shallow baths morning and evening, adding six drops of Tea Tree essential oil.

I have found this to be an effective treatment for many women who have suffered with this problem, resolving the abscess within a few days.

It is important to seek medical advice if the infection does not respond to this treatment within a day or two. Once the abscess has cleared, I would recommend that you continue to use 4 drops of Tea Tree oil in the bath for several weeks to help prevent reinfection of the glands. You can use other essential oils at the same time, but keep the total number of drops to six.

CYSTITIS

This is an inflammation inside the bladder, usually due to a bacterial infection. Sometimes vaginal deodorants and perfumed soap can cause an allergic reaction and result in an attack of cystitis. Non-bacterial infections such as Thrush can also lead to cystitis.

The symptoms of cystitis are easy to recognise. They include a burning or scalding pain when passing urine. There is an urgent need to pass urine several times each hour with very small amounts of urine being passed. Some women complain of lower abdominal aches, lower back pain and a high temperature, the urine may be cloudy or blood stained. These latter symptoms require urgent medical treatment.

Prevention is better than cure

If you have a tendency to cystitis drink at least one to two litres of water each day. Always go to the toilet when you need to rather than leaving the urine in the bladder to stagnate.

After sexual intercourse go to the toilet to pass urine then wash yourself. Avoid using perfumed soaps and vaginal deodorants.

When bathing always add an essential oil such as Tea Tree, Sandalwood, Cypress or Bergamot to the bath, a total of six drops is needed.

Self help for an attack of cystitis

First drink lots of water, at least $\frac{1}{4}$ of a litre every half an hour. Some women have found that drinking Cranberry juice helps as it makes the urine less acidic and therefore makes a less favourable environment in which bacteria can multiply. The commonest bacterium responsible for cystitis is the E Coli and this cannot multiply in alkaline urine. Take shallow baths at least three times during the first day of the onset of attack. The essential oils to add to the bath are six drops of either Bergamot, Tea Tree or Sandalwood.

Make an antiseptic solution with which to swab the vaginal area gently after urinating. Take one litre of mineral water to which you add 2 drops of bergamot essential oil. Swab the genital area from the front to the back using fresh cotton wool each time. Never use the same piece of cotton wool twice. Prepare a massage blend using Chamomile, Lavender and Bergamot and massage the lower back and abdomen every four hours, this will ease the pain. The following blend is not only analgesic it is also an excellent antiseptic for urinary tract infections.

To make use 20 mls of a carrier oil

Add	Chamomile	3 drops
	Lavender	5 drops
	Bergamot	2 drops

You should always seek medical advice as soon as possible, as you may require antibiotics. Self help aromatherapy can be continued to support any medical treatment.

Relaxation: Try to relax your mind as well as your body. Vaporise a calming essential oil such as Lavender, Mandarin, Chamomile or Geranium. Lie down and enjoy a good book whilst you are following your self help treatment.

THRUSH

Thrush is caused by a yeast-like fungus called Candida Albicans. Many people have Candida Albicans on their skin, mouth and in their bowels. It is harmless most of the time, and we are not aware of its presence. When it multiplies it can get out of control and can cause the problem known as Thrush. This can commonly affect the vagina and the vulva. It makes its presence known by creating intense itching and sometimes a thick white vaginal discharge which looks a bit like cottage cheese. It can irritate the vulval area and cause it to swell making it painful to pass urine.

Thrush thrives in moist, damp, warm conditions. It is best to avoid taking baths when suffering with this condition, have showers instead or very brief cool baths.

Thrush can occur during pregnancy because there is an increased level of oestrogen making a favourable environment for yeasts to grow.

Antibiotics kill off friendly organisms in the body, but in the process of destroying alien bacteria, they can disturb the balance of other micro organisms leaving more space in which yeasts can grow and set up infections. Some women suffer from thrush following a course of antibiotics. In order to prevent this occurring a month's course of Acidophilus Lactobacilli capsules should be taken. Lactobacilli are healthy bacteria which are present throughout the body and help to keep Candida in the vagina under control. Lactobacilli affect the glycogen in the vaginal secretions and convert it into lactic acid thus helping to create a more acidic environment in which Candida cannot thrive. The Lactobacilli also help to re-establish the good intestinal flora that the antibiotics have disrupted. Eating plenty of live unpasturised yoghurt can have the same effect.

Yeasts are more likely to cause an infection if you are run down or suffering from stress.

Broken skin around the vulval area is an ideal spot in which yeasts can grow and flourish.

Thrush can be sexually transmitted, therefore if a woman is suffering from thrush and she has a partner, it is important that both parties are treated to prevent reinfection occurring. If in doubt as to the cause of the symptoms then it is best for both you and your partner to seek medical advice.

Self help treatment for the relief of thrush
Aromatherapy consists of local applications to the genital area.

Purchase a 450 gram tub of plain unpasturised yoghurt, open four of the acidophalus capsules emptying the contents into the yoghurt and mixing well. Add three drops of Tea Tree oil. Soak a small size tampon in this mixture leaving the string free from the mixture. When it has expanded and absorbed some of the yoghurt mixture (this usually takes about half an hour) remove it from the tub and insert the tampon into the vagina. Wash your hands well before doing this. Leave it in place for one hour then remove it. Repeat this at least three times a day on the first day of the infection. In between using the tampons in this way, put some of the mixture around the vulva and inside the vagina, it is very soothing and helps to control the itching.

Continue this regime for two to three days by which time the infection should have cleared. (Do not use these tampons if you are pregnant.)

Diet plays an important role in self help treatment. Women who suffer with thrush should follow an anti-Candida diet which is low in yeasts and sugars.

Foods to avoid are: Breads, pasties, cottage cheese, mushrooms, vinegar, cheeses, ice cream, peanuts, dates, figs, prunes, raisins, olives, chocolate, honey, sugar, salad dressings and fruit juices. Consult a nutritionist if you want further advice.

Once the attack is under control continue with the diet for at least a month. When you take a bath add a few drops of Tea Tree essential oil to it as this is antifungal and will help to prevent further attacks. Avoid wearing nylon underwear and tight jeans as these trap the heat and create an environment in which yeasts thrive.

VAGINAL DISCHARGE

Most women will experience some slight vaginal discharge which has no odour, this is normal and nothing to worry about. It usually starts several months before a girl has her first period when the gradually increasing levels of oestrogen begin to stimulate the oestrogen sensitive vaginal cells causing an increase in cervical mucous and the rate of cell renewal in the vagina. The amount of vaginal discharge will vary throughout the menstrual cycle. When a discharge begins to cause irritation, discomfort or an unpleasant odour you should consult your doctor.

VAGINITIS

Vaginitis is inflammation of the vagina, usually due to organisms such as Candida Albicans and Trichomonas. Vaginitis can occur with hormonal changes leading up to the menopause. The vagina can become dry and the skin easily irritated, causing infection. The symptoms of a vaginal infection are itching, burning, an unpleasant odour and usually a change in vaginal discharge.

TRICHOMONAS VAGINALIS

This infection is caused by a protozoan parasite which causes inflammation of the vagina in women and urethritis in men. It affects the genito-urinary system and it is possible to contract it from a lavatory seat, or a moist towel which is harbouring the organism.

The symptoms are; the vagina and vulva are painful and irritated and emit a thin foamy discharge which is white or a greenish yellow in colour and is offensive in odour. If the urethra is also affected it will cause a burning pain when urine is passed. It is important to have medical treatment for this condition.

Aromatherapy treatments: Take warm baths to which you add 3 drops of Lavender and 3 drops of Tea Tree essential oils. Relax in the bath for ten to fifteen minutes. Taking these baths can complement any medical treatment.

If the infection is caused by Candida Albicans, then follow the self help treatment for Thrush.

NON INFECTIVE LEUCORRHOEA

This condition occurs when there is a proliferation of old dead cells being passed out through the vagina with the usual vaginal secretions. The discharge is normally white and may be irritating and can sometimes attract bacteria and lead to infection. If this condition persists a woman should seek medical advice as a heavy vaginal discharge, particularly if it is offensive, can be a warning that there might be an underlying problem that needs investigating.

Taking daily baths with the addition of essential oils such as Bergamot, Sandalwood, Tea Tree and Cypress (all of which are antiseptic and bactericidal) can help to prevent infection occurring. Add a total of six drops of essential oil to every bath. These oils have an affinity for the genito-urinary system and are therefore good friends for many feminine conditions.

GENITAL HERPES

These are two types of Herpes Simplex virus.

Type 1 which causes cold sores around the mouth and nose, but rarely in the genital area.

Herpes Simplex type 2 can cause sores in the genital and anal area and sometimes on the mouth. It is possible to transfer the herpes infection from the mouth to the genital area.

The symptoms of Genital Herpes are stinging, tingling and itching around the genitals.

Small blisters form which burst leaving small red ulcers that are very painful, especially when passing urine.

The herpes can occur when a woman is run down or suffering from stress. Sometimes they can occur during the menstrual cycle.

Aromatherapy treatment, as in many other cases, can complement medical treatment.

It is important to avoid sexual intercourse if suffering from a herpes infection until the condition has healed.

Washing the genital area with a solution containing essential oils can be soothing and help to prevent secondary infection occurring.

Take a one litre bottle of mineral water, add four drops of tea tree and four drops of Bergamot essential oils and shake well. Use this to wash the genital area each time after going to the toilet. Wash from the front to the back using fresh cotton wool each time.

Take cool shallow baths to which you add three drops of Tea Tree and three drops of Bergamot essential oil; these baths are soothing on the genitals. Continue this treatment until the sores have healed.

Herpes of the Mouth

Once again these can flare up whenever a woman is run down, stressed or suffering from a cold or influenza. At the first sign of a cold sore, which is usually signalled by a tingling sensation around the site where the herpes is trying to develop, dab neat Tea Tree onto the area using a cotton bud. Repeat this every three hours. In many cases this simple treatment can prevent the outbreak. Make sure that you dab the Tea Tree on the affected site and not on unaffected skin as it may irritate. If you are unable to start this treatment straight away, do so as soon as possible, it is effective in preventing the development of blisters.

7 | Aromatherapy and infertility

The trauma that infertility can cause to a couple can be extremely stressful. We, as women, assume that at some stage in our lives we may decide to have a baby. So when a woman finds she is having difficulty conceiving the emotional turmoil that ensues can be difficult to cope with.

To help the mind and body relax vaporise calming essential oils. Lavender and Geranium can be of immense value at such times.

Approximately 20% of infertility has an unknown cause. Some of the factors that can affect female fertility are:

Endometriosis
Irregular ovulation
Pelvic infection that has caused scarring of the fallopian tubes
Weak immune system, for example making antibodies against the sperm of some men
Stress

Many couples decide to undergo Invitro-fertilisation (IVF) treatment which offers real hope of a pregnancy. This involves a great deal of tenacity on the part of the couple, as there are numerous investigations and treatments. Women in particular can feel as if life has been put on hold. It can be a stressful time for the couple and lead to an unnatural and clinical love life.

The treatment is uncompromising. Women can experience high levels of anxiety, loss of self esteem, a feeling of failure and unhappiness. Anxiety and stress can antagonise the situation for both men and women.

Aromatherapy can help to relieve the strain and tension, allowing the mind and body to relax which is conducive to conception.

If undergoing IVF treatment both the man and woman will benefit from regular aromatherapy massage. The massage could be given two to three days prior to any other treatment thus ensuring optimum relaxation prior to the medical treatment.

Couples can benefit from massaging one another with relaxing sensuous oils such as Neroli, Orange, Bergamot and Ylang Ylang. Make it a general practice to vaporise essential oils in your home, this will have a calming influence on your mind. Use oils such as Lavender, Mandarin and Bergamot and take regular aromatic relaxing baths with any of the oils mentioned above. (Please remember that any of the citrus oils can be skin irritants therefore use them in low dosage.)

Suggested massage blends

Carrier oil 20 mls
Add   Bergamot   1 drop
        Neroli   3 drops

Nerolis is potent and expensive and should be used in minute amounts.

Carrier oil 20 mls
Add   Bergamot   5 drops
        Orange   2 drops
        Ylang Ylang 3 drops

Another very helpful aid is the use of the Flower Remedies. These gentle and benign remedies can help to lift negative emotional states of mind so restoring calm and balance.

8 | Aromatherapy and pregnancy

Here are some useful tips for pregnant women on the safe use of aromatherapy for some of the common discomforts that can be experienced during pregnancy. For more detailed information I would recommend the reader consult a book that deals exclusively with aromatherapy and pregnancy and of course follow whatever clinical or medical advice is available.

There are a number of essential oils that should *not* be used during pregnancy.

Avoid emmenagogue oils as these encourage menstruation. Others are considered too stimulating and there is the danger that they may cross the placental barrier. Many Aromatherapists use Lavender during pregnancy even though it is an emmenagogue oil as it is very mild. I use it after the 12th week of pregnancy in a very low dosage.

If there is any history of abnormal bleeding or past miscarriages then even lavender should be avoided.

If you are pregnant and would like to use essential oils it is always advisable to consult a professional aromatherapist for expert advice as to the choice of oils and how they can be beneficial for you.

The benefits of aromatherapy during pregnancy are numerous. It aids relaxation and helps the mother to be able to cope better during labour.

Ligaments supporting large muscles become stretched during pregnancy causing tired and aching muscles. Massage can help to alleviate these aches and pains and restore the tonicity of the muscles.

Massage encourages physical and emotional relaxation and will therefore complement and reinforce any relaxation techniques that are learnt during antenatal classes.

It also helps to tone and moisturise the skin, thus minimising stretch marks.

Essential oils to avoid during pregnancy
Angelica, Aniseed, Arnica, Basil, Camphor, Cypress, Cedarwood, Clary Sage, Clove, Cinnamon, Fennel, Hyssop, Jasmin, Juniper, Lovage, Melissa, Myrrh, Marjoram, Origanum, Parsley, Peppermint, Rosemary, Rose, Savory, Sage, Spanish Marjoram, Sweet Marjoram, Tarragon, Thyme.

Essential oils to avoid for the first twelve weeks of pregnancy

If there is any history of bleeding or miscarriage then do not use these oils throughout the pregnancy: Chamomile Roman, Rose centifolia and damascena, Geranium, Lavender.

Dosage of essential oils during pregnancy

Aromatherapists work on a 1¼% dilution when treating pregnant women. This is half the adult dose for normal use.
For example:
To 20 mls of a carrier oil add 5 drops of essential oil.
To 50 mls carrier oil add 12 drops of essential oil.
To 100 mls carrier oil add 25 drops of essential oil.
It is important not to exceed the stated amount of essential oil especially during pregnancy. (See formula for blending instructions on pages 14–15)

How Aromatherapy can give comfort and help during pregnancy

Helping to prevent stretch marks

Anti-Stretch Mark Oil

Sweet Almond oil	40 mls
Avocado oil	10 mls
Add Mandarin essential oil	12 drops

Apply a small amount to the areas which are prone to stretching and gently massage into the skin daily. These areas are usually the buttocks, thighs, breasts, hips and abdomen. I would recommend that you continue to use this oil for at least three months after the birth.

Sore Breasts

Always ensure you have a properly fitting bra which gives good support. Wear it in bed if your breasts are particularly heavy and uncomfortable. Use the anti–stretch mark oil on the breasts daily.

Preparing the Perineal Area

This is the area of skin between the vagina and the anus. During labour it will be stretched extensively. Moisturising this area daily throughout the pregnancy can often help to prevent the necessity of an episiotomy during birth. An episiotomy is the incision made into the peritoneum during childbirth to prevent the mother being torn. The episiotomy is stitched up after birth.

To prepare the perineum gently rub a little Jojoba oil or sweet Almond oil into the perineal area daily, this will ensure it becomes supple and can stretch with ease.

Indigestion and Heartburn

This is quite common in later pregnancy. Gently massage the area between the breasts and the top of the abdomen to help alleviate discomfort.

Use carrier oil 5 mls Sweet Almond oil
Add   Mandarin oil   1 drop

Aches and pains around the shoulders and back

All women enjoy gentle massage given by their partner or a friend during pregnancy. The mother should lie on her side or sit astride a chair well supported with pillows, whichever is the most comfortable for her.

Use gentle upward strokes, being especially gentle massaging the lower back.

The same massage blend can be used as for anti-stretch marks.

Insomnia

Insomnia can be a problem in later months of pregnancy, especially when the baby is kicking. Vaporise lavender in the bedroom by adding two drops to a vaporiser.

Helping to prevent Varicose Veins

See chapter on maintaining good health Promoting Good Circulation. Do not use the suggested oils under this heading for massage whilst you are pregnant instead use:

Massage Blend: Carrier oil 20 mls
Add   Mandarin   5 drops

Essential oils for Labour

Your partner or a friend can be a great comfort during the early stages of labour giving gentle back massage between contractions to ease pain.

If you are planning to use aromatherapy during your labour, it is a good idea to have your oils mixed and packed in your bag in case you have to leave for the hospital in a hurry.

Some of the most useful oils are Jasmine, Rose, Lavender and Neroli. Select an oil which you particularly like and have it blended by your aromatherapist. If you prefer to do this yourself the following blends are suitable.

Labour massage oil
Sweet Almond oil 50 mls
Add   12 drops   either Rose, Jasmine, Neroli or
Lavender

It is always a good idea for your partner to have some massage practice before the big day. This will ensure he or she feels confident once labour gets under way.

Perfuming the labour room with essential oils that are uplifting and refreshing such as Lemon, Bergamot and Mandarin. To do this fill a bowl with hot water add 6 drops of the essential oil. This should then ideally be placed on a radiator. Alternatively use one of the vaporisers that work from an electric point; in this case the essential oils are dropped on to a filter pad fitted to the base of the vaporiser. Once switched on the essential oils are vaporised into the atmosphere.

Post Natal Aromatherapy

Healing the Perineum

If you have had an episiotomy. The oils will help with healing and prevent infection.

Fill the bath with warm water, add 2 drops of Lavender and 2 drops of Tea Tree, relax and soak for ten to fifteen minutes. Take this bath morning and evening.

Sore Nipples

Sore nipples can occur following breast feeding. To prevent soreness start to prepare your nipples approximately two to three weeks before the baby is due. Each day gently massage some Calendula cream into them. Following the birth continue to use the Calendula cream in between breast feeding.

Ensure that you wash and dry your nipples carefully before breast feeding your baby.

Baby Blues

Many women feel tired and "weepy" for a day or two after having a baby. This is due to the fluctuating hormone levels. To help cope with this give yourself time to relax. When the baby is sleeping take a lovely relaxing bath using essential oils. Select from Bergamot, Lavender, Geranium, Rose, Mandarin, Neroli and Petitgrain using a total of six drops of any one or any combination of six drops.

Vaporise uplifting oils such as Bergamot, Orange, Lemon and Petitgrain; mix a few of these together to create a relaxing atmosphere in your room. Then get your partner to massage your back.

Try using some of the Flower Remedies to suit the emotional state of mind you find yourself in.

The baby blues usually lasts a day or so, therefore it is important to seek medical help when there are prolonged feelings of despair, apathy, an inability to cope, repressed anger or guilt as this could be a sign of the more serious condition of post natal depression which needs urgent attention.

9 | Having a hysterectomy

There are many reasons why a woman may have a hysterectomy (surgical removal of the uterus commonly known as the womb).

Sometimes it can be a welcome relief, especially if prolonged and debilitating heavy bleeding has been your problem. On the other hand, there can be feelings of loss and sadness as a phase of your life is ended.

It is very important that you question your doctor's reasons for wanting to perform a hysterectomy. Don't just accept this as routine. Aim to make yourself as informed as possible on the subject and be sure that other methods of treatment have been considered before resorting to surgery. Having explored every avenue, you will be better prepared to make a decision and make a positive acceptance of the operation.

You are probably aware of many of the reasons why a hysterectomy is performed, nevertheless I will briefly outline the main reasons.

To treat extensive endometriosis

To remove large or multiple fibroids

To remove cancer of the vagina, cervix, uterus, fallopian tubes or ovaries

To treat an uncontrollable infection of the pelvis

To treat heavy vaginal bleeding that has failed to respond to treatment and is causing anaemia

To remove a prolapsed uterus

So having made your decision to have a hysterectomy let us try and make your stay in hospital as smooth as possible.

Going into hospital

There are a number of things that you can do to prepare yourself. A positive outlook will make a big difference and help with a speedy recovery.

Here are a few general tips that can help you.

If you smoke, try hard to stop or at least reduce the number of cigarettes that you smoke, as smokers are more likely to develop a chest infection or a blood clot after surgery.

Plan to have an aromatherapy massage a week or so before you are due to go into hospital as this will help you relax and unwind; and as mentioned before, this can have many physical benefits. May I suggest that you read the section on 'Looking after your health with

Aromatherapy' as the topics covered will help you to prepare yourself for hospital.

Take one or two of your favourite essential oils into hospital with you, as you may be able to use them in your bath prior to the operation (it would be advisable to check with the ward sister first). Scent your bedlinen with Lavender to help promote relaxation. Ask your aromatherapist to prepare a body lotion with some of your favourite oils, this little luxury will help moisturise and keep your skin supple. (Use after your operation)

To help with the negative emotional feelings of worry and anxiety, use the appropriate Flower Remedies.

After the Operation

If you feel a bit "weepy" after the operation, remember this usually passes within a day or so. Share these feelings with your family, talking about them can be a relief in itself.

When you are home, cosset yourself by using your anti-depressant oils such as Lemon, Bergamot, Orange and Lemon as vaporisers, and treat yourself to a professional aromatherapy massage, you deserve it. Make time each day to have a relaxing aromatic bath.

For the first few days after the operation you will probably feel tired and your concentration may be poor. This is not unusual and is due partly to the response of your body to the stress of the operation and to the after effects of the anaesthetic which is still in your system. So take it easy and do not expect too much from yourself, if you feel tired then rest.

Nurture yourself by ensuring your diet contains lots of fresh fruit, vegetables and protein; these will help you regain your strength so that you can start doing some gentle exercises.

Sometimes, following a hysterectomy, a urinary tract infection can occur, or you may find you need to urinate a little more often than is usual. Don't worry about this. The bladder will gradually return to normal. You can use essential oils in your bath that have an affinity with the urinary tract and can help to prevent infection, such as Bergamot, Lavender, Tea Tree and Sandalwood. Six drops in total (any one or two oils) added to your bath.

Once your scar is well healed, gently massage a blend of sweet Almond oil and Mandarin essential oil into the scar line daily. This will ease any tightening around the skin and help the scar to fade.

If you go out to work, you will probably feel ready to return within six to eight weeks following your operation but continue using aromatherapy oils to keep you in top form.

QUICK EASY GUIDE TO THE USE OF ESSENTIAL OILS FOR PHYSICAL CONDITIONS

Methods of use:
B – bath; M – massage; C – compress; V – vaporisation; I – inhalation; G – gargle; L – lotion

Digestive System	Method of use	Essential oil
Bloatedness	B M C	Peppermint, Ginger
Indigestion	B M C	Peppermint, Orange
Diarrhoea	B M C	Chamomile, Lavender
Nausea	M V	Ginger, Lemon, Peppermint
Mouth Ulcer	G	Tea Tree
Oral Thrush	G	Tea Tree
Gastric colic	M C	Lavender, Ginger, Mandarin

Circulatory system		
Cold hand/feet	B M L	Ginger, Marjoram
Chilblains	B M L	Ginger, Lavender
Haemorrhoids	B	Cypress, Lemon
Varicose veins	B C L	Cypress, Lemon
Hypertension	M B	Lavender, Ylang Ylang
Cramp	B M L	Marjoram, Ginger
Palpitations	B M V	Lavender

Respiratory System		
Coughs	B M V I	Benzoin, Eucalyptus, Sandalwood
Asthma	V M	Cypress, Frankincense
Sore Throat	M V I L	Benzoin Lemon
	G	Tea Tree
Sinusitis	V I M	Eucalyptus, Lavender
Bronchitis	M V I	Eucalyptus, Tea Tree, Lavender
Laryngitis	I V L	Lavender
Hayfever	V I	Eucalyptus

Muscles/Joints		
Muscular strain	M B C L	Lavender, Bergamot, Rosemary
Rheumatoid Arthritis	B M C L	Chamomile, Lavender
Osteoarthritis	B M C L	Lavender, Rosemary, Black Pepper, Ginger
Muscular spasm	B M C L	Black pepper, Lavender, Bergamot, Rosemary, Chamomile
Repetitive Strain Injury	B M L	Rosemary, Lavender, Bergamot

Immune system		
Colds/Flu	B M C	Lavender, Tea Tree, Lemon
	V I	Eucalyptus, Sandalwood
Cold sore	Neat	Tea Tree

Skin disorders

Acne	B C V L	Tea Tree, Bergamot, Lemon, Geranium, Rosemary, Lavender
Eczema	C/Lotion	Roman Chamomile
Psoriasis	Lotion	Carrot seed, Bergamot
Boils	C V	Tea Tree, Lavender, Bergamot
Cellulite	B M L	Rosemary, Juniper, Lemon
Veruccas	B L	Tea Tree, Lemon
Warts	B	Tea Tree, Lemon
Cuts/Grazes	B	Tea Tree, Lavender, Niaouli
Insect bites	B C	Lavender
Sunburn	B C Lotion	Lavender, Chamomile
Prickly heat	B Lotion	Lavender, Chamomile
Itchy skin	Lotion	Roman Chamomile, Lavender

Female reproductive system

Painful periods	B M C	Lavender, Ginger, Chamomile
Heavy periods	B M C	Rose, Frankincense, Geranium
Irregular periods	B M C	Rose, Geranium, Lavender
PMT	B M C V	Geranium, Lavender, Chamomile
Menopause	B M V	Geranium, Lavender, Rose, Frankinsence

Genito/Urinary system

Bed wetting	B M	Cypress
Cystitis	B M C	Bergamot, Tea Tree, Sandalwood
Genital Herpes	B	Tea Tree, Bergamot
Thrush	Sitz bath	Tea Tree
Vaginitis	B M	Bergamot, Lavender, Sandalwood

Nervous system

Headache	B M V C	Lavender, Peppermint
Stress/Anxiety	B M C	Lavender, Bergamot, Clary Sage
Exhaustion	B M V	Lavender, Clary Sage
Insomnia	B M V	Lavender, Chamomile
Grief	B M V	Lavender, Rose
Poor concentration	V	Rosemary, Grapefruit, Peppermint
Restlessness	B M V	Lavender
Irritability	B V	Lavender, Geranium

Envoi

Remember it is not selfish to look after your body; carried out without fuss it could be the most unselfish act you ever do.

Through your healthy, happy, relaxed and responsive body you can bring help and harmony to others and, through tranquillity tune in to their thoughts and needs.

Don't be overwhelmed by all the medical words in the book just use and enjoy your special oils.

Ann

OTHER BOOKS FROM AMBERWOOD PUBLISHING ARE:

Aromatherapy – A Guide for Home Use by Christine Westwood. All you need to know about essential oils and using them. £1.99.

Aromatherapy – For Stress Management by Christine Westwood. Covering the use of essential oils for everyday stress-related problems. £2.99.

Aromatherapy – For Healthy Legs and Feet by Christine Westwood. A comprehensive guide to the use of essential oils for the treatment of legs and feet, including illustrated massage instructions. £2.99.

Aromatherapy – Simply For You by Marion Del Gaudio Mak. A clear, simple and comprehensive guide to Aromatherapy for beginners. £1.99.

Aromatherapy – A Nurses Guide by Ann Percival SRN. This book draws on the author's medical skills and experience as a qualified aromatherapist to provide the ultimate, safe, lay guide to the natural benefits of Aromatherapy. Including recipes and massage techniques for many medical conditions and a quick reference chart. £2.99.

Aroma Science – The Chemistry & Bioactivity of Essential Oils by Dr Maria Lis-Balchin. With a comprehensive list of the Oils and scientific analysis – a must for all with an interest in the science of Aromatherapy. Includes sections on methodology, the sense of smell and the history of Aromatherapy. £4.99.

Plant Medicine – A Guide for Home Use (New Edition) by Charlotte Mitchell MNIMH. A guide to home use giving an insight into the wonderful healing qualities of plants. £2.99.

Woman Medicine – Vitex Agnus Castus by Simon Mills MA, FNIMH. The wonderful story of the herb that has been used for centuries in the treatment of women's problems. £2.99.

Ancient Medicine – Ginkgo Biloba (New Edition) by Dr Desmond Corrigan BSc(Pharms), MA, Phd, FLS, FPSI. Improved memory, circulation and concentration are associated in this book with medicine from this fascinating tree. £2.99.

Indian Medicine – The Immune System by Dr Desmond Corrigan BSc(Pharms), MA, Phd, FLS, FPSI. An intriguing account of the history and science of the plant called Echinacea and its power to influence the immune system. £2.99.

Herbal Medicine for Sleep & Relaxation by Dr Desmond Corrigan BSc(Pharms), MA, PhD, FLS, FPSI. An expertly written guide to the natural sedatives as an alternative to orthodox drug therapies, drawing on the latest medical research, presented in an easy reference format. £2.99.

Herbal First Aid by Andrew Chevallier BA, MNIMH. A beautifully clear reference book of natural remedies and general first aid in the home. £2.99.

Natural Taste – Herbal Teas, A Guide for Home Use by Andrew Chevallier BA, MNIMH. This charmingly illustrated book contains a comprehensive compendium of Herbal Teas gives information on how to make it, its benefits, history and folklore. £2.99.

Garlic– How Garlic Protects Your Heart by Prof E. Ernst MD, PhD. Used as a medicine for over 4500 years, this book examines the latest scientific evidence supporting Garlic's effect in reducing cardiovascular disease, the Western World's number one killer. £3.99.

Insomnia – Doctor I Can't Sleep by Dr Adrian Williams FRCP. Written by one of the world's leading sleep experts, Dr Williams explains the phenomenon of sleep and sleeping disorders and gives advice on treatment. With 25% of the adult population reporting difficulties sleeping – this book will be essential reading for many. £2.99.

Signs & Symptoms of Vitamin Deficiency by Dr Leonard Mervyn BSc, PhD, C.Chem, FRCS. A home guide for self diagnosis which explains and assesses Vitamin Therapy for the prevention of a wide variety of diseases and illnesses. £2.99.

Causes & Prevention of Vitamin Deficiency by Dr Leonard Mervyn BSc, PhD, C.Chem, FRCS. A home guide to the Vitamin content of foods and the depletion caused by cooking, storage and processing. It includes advice for those whose needs are increased due to lifestyle, illness etc. £2.99.

Eyecare Eyewear – For Better Vision by Mark Rossi Bsc, MBCO. A complete guide to eyecare and eyewear including an assessment of the types of spectacles and contact lenses available and the latest corrective surgical procedures. £3.99.

Lm   6/11